GARBAGE GIRL

POEMS

by

MAMTA

notionpress.com

INDIA · SINGAPORE · MALAYSIA

Copyright © Mamta Sunil Nagpal 2024
All Rights Reserved.

ISBN 979-8-89186-797-0

This book has been published with all efforts taken to make the material error-free after the consent of the author. However, the author and the publisher do not assume and hereby disclaim any liability to any party for any loss, damage, or disruption caused by errors or omissions, whether such errors or omissions result from negligence, accident, or any other cause.

While every effort has been made to avoid any mistake or omission, this publication is being sold on the condition and understanding that neither the author nor the publishers or printers would be liable in any manner to any person by reason of any mistake or omission in this publication or for any action taken or omitted to be taken or advice rendered or accepted on the basis of this work. For any defect in printing or binding the publishers will be liable only to replace the defective copy by another copy of this work then available.

CONTENTS

THE NEW HOUSE 3
- Flagless Creature 4
- Silently, ... 6
- Belonging. Longing. Belonging. 7
- New Bondings 8
- Train Ride 9
- Walking into this Night 10
- Moods of Nature 12
- Bites 13
- The New House 14
- Three Sad Roommates 16
- Sad, Sad Girls in this Sad, Sad City 17
- Far Away 20
- The Missing Taste of Lemonade 21
- Howls of the Ecosystem 23
- Expanding Emptiness 25
- Shared Spaces and Colliding Worlds 26
- Drifting in the Unknown 27

AFTER THE ILLUMINATION 29
- DATE: 17/11/2021 30
- Loud Silences 31
- Patches 33
- Late October Welcomes the Void: 36
- Justice for Jared 38
- Looking for You 39
- DATE: 04/12/2021 40
- Goodbye Boyfriend 41

Separation in Space 42
Wintering in Vancouver... 43
When the Body Splinters into an Interstellar 45
After the Illumination 46
DATE: 25/11/2021.. 47
into the deep.. 48
In Time,.. 49

FUNERAL SEASON 50
The Light of Grief 51
Forgotten Days.. 53
Unearthing in Alleyways 55
Laughter Season 58
Where Do the Most Painful Cries Reside? 59
Scars of Two Cities 60
Existential Crisis 61
Poisoned Rats 62
I Can't Pick Myself Up.. 63
Hunger Games... 64
Eternal Decay 65
Nausea 66
Numbing 67
Burial Process 68
Grandma's Final Prime 69
I Smell Like the Whiff of a Hospital Bathroom,
    Covered in the Vomit of a Cancer Patient 70
Monstrous Urge 72
Funeral Season... 74
Two 75
Pat on Your Back... 77
incomplete circles... 78
Still Alive 79

एक दर्द ऐसा भी 81
ऐसा वक्त 82
ऐसा कैसे हो गया 84
खोयी खोयी 86
दर्द की बारिश 87
नाराजगी 88
बस हुआ अब 90
ऐ मन 91

NOTES & ACKNOWLEDGEMENTS 93

Mamta

*"I find my corneas stuck on an unborn flare in the alleyway.
I loathe the wailing of a baby; it makes me want to rip off my ears.
My kidney begs me to be hauled; I get a spine curvature disorder.
My nose pours crimson rain. Sometimes, green vomit cascades
from my mouth as my bone spikes out of my knee to protect me.
My existence unfurls crimson shame.*

My name is litter.

My name is thunder.

My name is...my name...

An illicit train.

My name is debris.

A perennial stain.

My name is, my name is my name, my name is...

What is my name?"

– Unearthing in Alleyways by Mamta

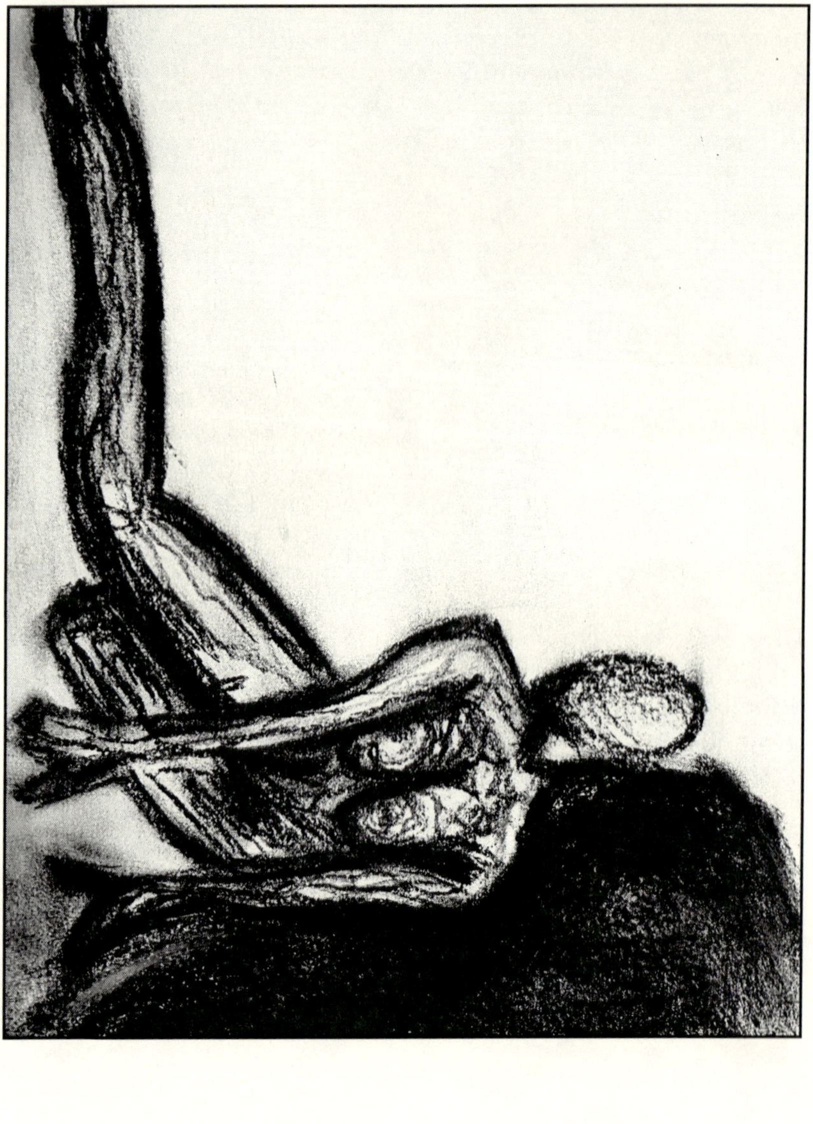

THE NEW HOUSE

"This is the grave and I'm turning into worms, horror of horrors! Satan, you clown, you want to dissolve me with your charms. Well, I want it. I want it! Stab me with a pitchfork, sprinkle me with fire."

- Night in Hell by Arthur Rimbaud

Flagless Creature

The colorless country flag flutters on my back, carrying the stings of an aggressive wind. I have always wondered what the color of my flag is. A mischievous seagull wages war with nasty crows in my colony.

I wonder where my colony begins. Everything ends. I believe it ends with a haul of vast longing. It doesn't begin with the vault of red roses nestling on my lips. Nor does it begin in the arms of my distant lovers.

I do know what it feels like when a departed pigeon feather plays seesaw in circles on my tanned thighs. I want to paint my hair peacock blue so that I can redeem myself like a splintered rock. Lest we forget about the blooming white roses that never bloomed in my backyard. Lest we forget about our distances and separation from our roots.

My flag is colorless. Hearts are muted in the corners of my stamped religion, crawling on my long arms, tagging along with the weight of being born inside a briefcase. The shrieks of a flagless girl echo in her new neighborhood.

Perhaps it begins where the roots of my imaginary cherry tree spring. I savor every drop of cherry wine, making love to my broken spine. It doesn't begin beneath my raspy throat. It doesn't begin at the borders of Vancouver or even Bombay.

My flag is uncertainty. My flag is the color of turquoise ocean and flooded melancholia. I am not an artist. I am but a darkest canvas, longing to dream of a flag and a dwelling beside an unknown being.

SUBMERGING

Silently,

my home saw me leave this time
    with no hopes of coming back,
        letting the traces of my footsteps
            galloping at midnight become
              a lingering memory.

She looks at me in dismay
    like she knows there is no way I would find
        another bay under these pale lights.

Like she knows there is no way
    I would find new desires or a maternal ray
        in man-made bricks and walls,
            and a fragrance that crawls in my body
              for two billion years.

Like she knows even if I come back after
    losing myself to multiple shelters,
        in multiple dimensions,
            I would still be welcomed.

But it would be different this time.
    After all, everything and everyone
        moves on.

Mamta

Belonging. Longing. Belonging.

Deviant roads wait hopelessly for a traveler
With a longing to belong, and to belong
Is to be born with an expiration date.

All this craving for unwanted friendships,
All this longing for one dreadful night,
All this waiting to explode like a raging dynamite,

And experiencing the forming of an emotion making
Swirls as if the storm is one of the weakest girls.
And then,
the ice melts if you taste it with—

An open sky is like a wound
On an unstitched heart that is longing
For belonging
And longing.

What is this thirst for human affection,
Cradling on my chest like a faint melody?
What is this taste of desire, a gray cloud?
What is this sound of a crunching heart
After I fall in the eyes of a dead star?
And their graveyard calls my name,
Like I belong to the dead ones,
Like I belong to the earth,
Like I belong to the lost.

New Bondings

Clouds are looking like pearls painted on the sky.
I think about the new home to those clouds on my street.
Am I missing a warm body beside me,
or does the water taste like a waterfall today?

Unless someone is waiting to hear my muted voice,
I melt in the fresh snow. I lie to myself
and love like birds love an open sky,
or a new galaxy embraces the first sip of a suppressed cry.

I have wandered a lot this year.
I have lost and lost and lost myself this year.
I am bonded with myself for life now.

Train Ride

Tonight,

under the moonless sky,
I board a train with ghosts.
Conversations form into bubbles
out of thin air. My eyes can't unsee
the tarnished scenery wiping by
outside the train window.

My corneas are glued to the metal floor,
as if it's awaiting an earthquake
to escape our never-ending prison door.
Crunching of car tires on a cement floor,
mixed with the sound of an electric guitar,
echoes in the luggage I carried
along with my limitations from home.

I become the red light at a traffic signal
as I pass through unfamiliar contours of smiles,
and giggles forming into fresh skies
beside brand-new strangers in Vancouver.

I become the longest train ride
and a fleeting sunset.
I used to be the widest smile
before the spicy whiff of a masala chai in Bombay.

These days, I become multiple things:

a broken branch, an unsatisfied moon,
a sinful sunset, an untuned instrument,
a skipped heartbeat,
the sweltering summer heat.

Walking into this Night

The night ignites,
Your perfume bites
On the back of my right shoulder,
My fingertips look a day older.
I haven't brushed my hair since
Last weekend.
I have been unaware of
The forest burns,
And how life is just a bleak end,
No returns.

Your breathing concerns me,
Tortures me.
As we walk into this night,
Life walks beside us in a fright.

Will we ever be free?
Will we ever be free
From our fears and wounds,
Broken grounds.
I still want to walk into this night,
To be found
By you.

Mamta

Your heartbeat scares me,
Tears me apart
From my own skin.
I follow an unknown hymn,
Chasing the horizon's rim,
Swimming in the frozen sea,
To drink numbness,
Brokenness,
My heart is a big pile of mess.

The night lies,
Your smile multiplies,
My body dies
A million times,
As the night ignites,
Your perfume bites
On the back of my right shoulder.

Moods of Nature

Moods of nature is an eternal ache,
looking for internal connection with
clementine skies and thunderstorms.

Without the human race,
it would have been impossible
to know the color of the sun's face.

Prayers – I have recently encountered
hypnotic azure skies, but the exuberant heat
of my old city left burns
on my weakened heartbeat.

I have finally decided to die multiple times
rather than waste my one life
living in dull paradigms.

I stare back at the obscure shadows
as they stare back at me.
I ask questions of survival to
my neighborhood trees.
"How do you manage to shine
when the ruthless breeze slaps on your face?"
Tell me your ways.

I ask about my birth and my existence.
Why am I so distant and inconsistent?
I am a mess in this game of no-rule chess.

Moods of nature is chained to my skin.
Without shadows, there would be no deaths, no "I",
we shall meet in bottomless depths.

Mamta

Bites

The cold is biting me tonight,
Like the mosquitos in my old city, I've hated.
The solitary nights I've dated.
I've come this far to escape this pain,
But, one way or another,
I always find my way to destined train,
And I end up in the window seat,
To feel the cold
That is biting me
Tonight.

The New House

The new house is just bricks and walls
That crawl under your skin
Like a mortal sin.
She's a horror that never leaves your mind
Even if you're drugged
All the time.

You loathe for her temptation,
You crave for her affection.
Even a new house can be addictive
Like the drug you thought was vindictive,
And you always wanted to try,
But you didn't for a long time,
Because you were scared that she will brainwash you,
And erase the memory of your HOME.

So, you live your life in monochrome,
Pass your days in a house made of bones,
Until she summons the living.
You move from one,
To another,
And another,
But trust me, you won't find your mother
In this new house,
She's waiting for you
At home.

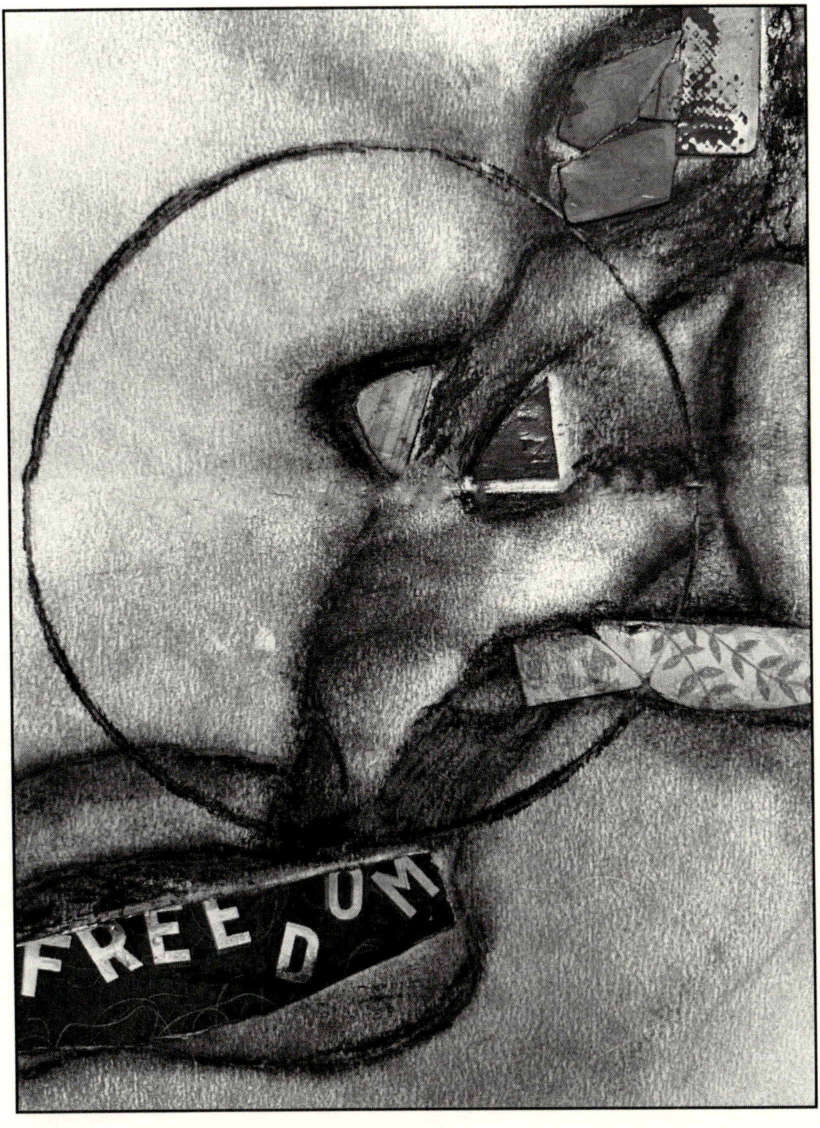
FREEDUM

Three Sad Roommates

She cried for one-third of her day. Daylight wounds her.
Ghosts stood with her. The night stood her up. With wired-faces
needling her toes, she finds herself consumed by the fumes
of forbidden fate with love.

> She got soaked up in the rain today. She walked for hours
> towards the skyline.
> Throwing knives is a hobby; no music came to her. No
> music came to any musician today.

I, a sleepless poet, sleeps knowing she is alive. And she is alive.
We exist.

Sad, Sad Girls in this Sad, Sad City

On her way to a sad, sad dinner date, she allowed sadness to follow them. She looked like a miserable spring after two months of an extended winter. The winds were roaring on the top of her bed in the midst of May. She longed to dance on the stage once more. Do you remember the sensation of your bare, tiny feet touching the wooden stage? She was a little girl once, too. She thought she was a little girl once. With curly hair. Very fair. Eyes, black. Black ice. Multiple lies.

Attachment has always been her biggest flaw. There is nothing in the world that she didn't get attached to, yet she felt so detached from everything. They talked about pink cats, pink shoes, pink skies, and something about pink lies with their pink eyes. They were sad, sad girls.

Finally, the sun knocked on her door today, but she couldn't answer because she was far away from the town. She was in the woods waiting for the wolves to have dinner with them. The sun didn't move for a long time. It stood stubborn on her door. She was away. She had always been away, since the day she was born. She didn't feel like she was born at all. She was born on January 1st, she thought. She thinks she was born on January 1st. She was born away. She doesn't know the name of the hospital, but it's away. The sun is a stubborn bitch. There's a glitch in this system of existence. She wanted to have dinner like a grown-up with another grown-up, but she was far, far away.

Garbage Girl

Her friend wept in silence. Where do you find your refuge? She has been looking for a cave to hide. She wept and wept and wept, silently. Where do you disappear? She has been looking for a tunnel to disappear into. Let's disappear and reappear, away. For they were sad, sad girls in this sad, sad city.

She never knew what honesty was, yet she was the most honest person she knew. Are you the most honest person you know? She was honest once, she thought. She thought she was honest once. Her friend has been sad lately, but she didn't know the reason for her sadness. She didn't understand sadness. He sat in their bedroom, beneath their bedside table, hiding his tail, staring deeply into the guts of their decorative wall with his glowing laser eyes. She couldn't hide herself these days. She had been waiting for someone to cloak her in their arms, so that she could sleep in the space far away.

But no one came. People had their fair share of problems. Why would anyone come to dinner with sadness? They were sad, sad girls in this sad, sad city. He came to devour them at their sad, sad dinner date. The gate is open now. It's never going to end. Sadness is just their friend now.

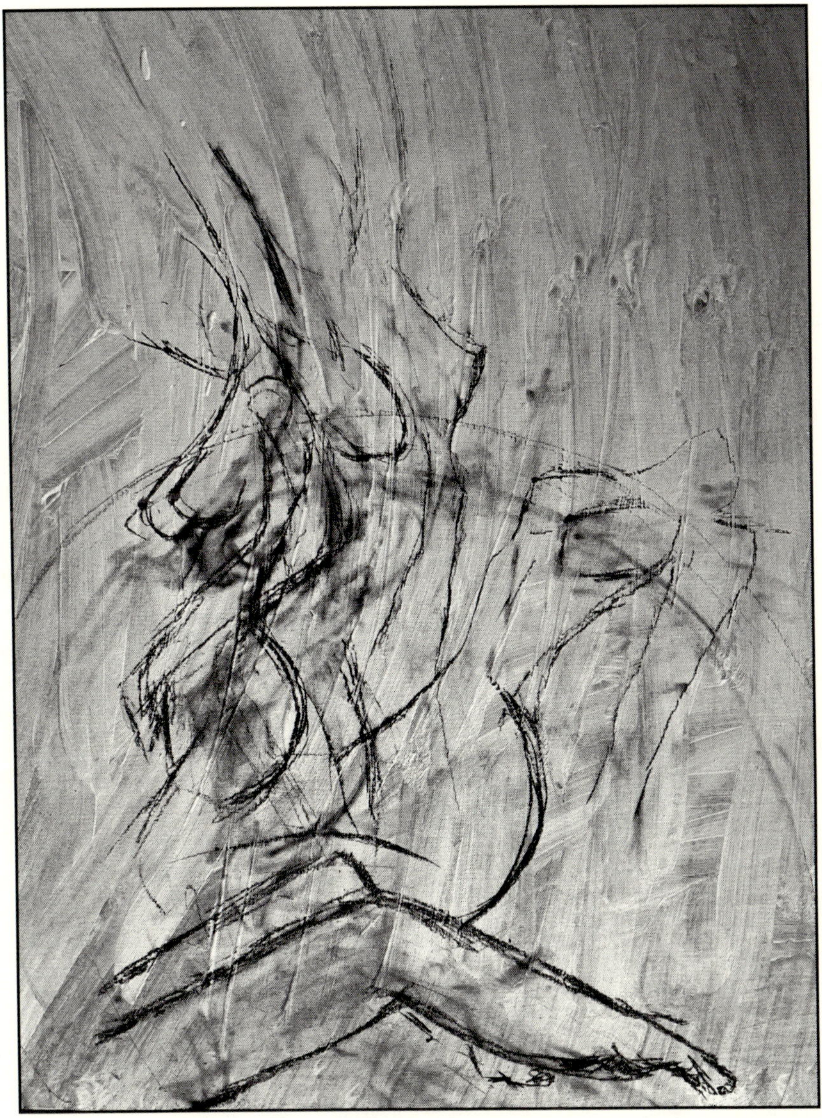

Far Away

The fragrance of my Ma's food
Lingers in my mind,
Like the scent of coconut oil—
Warm,
Vintage,
Unforgettable.
I remember, she asked me
To stay.
I boarded like an empty crate,
Left,
Right,
And straight.
To seek God
Like a fraud.
Every part of my history now hides,
My Ma calls me a mystery.
She lingers in my mind.
I am born blind,
I am born far, far away.

Mamta

The Missing Taste of Lemonade

Mornings feel like a storm in my bedroom.
I cover myself under a broken shade,
I squeeze my body in fear like my Ma
squeezes lemons every year.

I don't taste like lemonade anymore.
Life has changed.
Mornings are still rough to me
like a cold-blooded animal
sucking your soul for breakfast.
I despise the sound of breakfast,
But morning eats me as if I am
it's favorite meal of the day.

What do I taste like?

Do I taste like bitter orange juice?
Or an undercooked egg?
I don't taste like granulated sugar.
I am not dead yet.
People snicker at me
As if I am a red bird
Carrying fleas in my mouth.

What do I taste like?

Garbage Girl

My Ma used to tell me I taste
like her favorite Chaat– the mix of sweet and spicy.
But she doesn't eat her favorite food anymore.
This morning told me, I taste
like a burnt toast and rotten fruits
in the refrigerator today.
My Ma thinks I taste like frozen meal these days.
And I think they are all right.

Mamta

Howls of the Ecosystem

Roaring, whirling,
banging screams are heard
in the nights here.

I dissolve into the wooden floor,
hide some of my hands and feet
in the corner of a stranger's home.
My feet are sore from living,
from trying to survive in this world
where we don't know how to live.

Drops and drops, I swim in the lake
of sorrows and horrors,
flowing with vomit-green streams
that run under ruptured houses.
We wait to be choked by the hands
of a living ghost.
I killed some mosquitoes to roast for lunch.
Where do we hide this time?

The windowsill is frozen in May.
My eyes gallop inside the stillness
circulating in this foreign world.
A flooding abdomen and fear,
I fear too.
I fear as I spread fear,
I fear as I offer fear,
I fear as I engulf fear.
Fear is my dead mother.
I might see her in the morning
if she doesn't fear the sun rising
on this strange, bulbous sphere.
I don't want to hear your secrets,

Garbage Girl

I promise.

Where do we hide this time?

Streetlamps scream scarlet tonight,
just like the venom I gulped to taste this life.
A peculiar scream, I can hear somewhere in my eyes.
We celebrate a feeling of death lingering
in our bowels
while struggling to live.
Our time is short.
Shorter than plants and my neighboring red ants.
What do you fear?
Where will you hide this time?

Behind the edges of beyond and fire,
we hide under the wilderness
while we build our own pyre.
It's a curious place, I assure you.
I have seen it in my dreams.
Dreaming makes me feel barren.
I think I am attracted to dying more
than living
and that's why I am molded in the color of scare.
My claws are sore from building roofs.
The eighth one is still weaving sunbeams
before diminishing squeals surrender
from our past.
We are trapped in a graveyard
of my newly built web at last.
You kill me. I kill you.
The ecosystem breathes now.

Mamta

Expanding Emptiness

I feel empty,
so empty when you fill me up,

I expand
like Jupiter under Saturn.

I always hate myself after feeling
geometrical patterns,
igniting lanterns
between my thighs.

It's like a part of me wants to know
if I don't deserve to feel an outer space
revolving under my belly even for a single night.

And the other part of me feels
like I deserve to experience planets, universes,
storms and tornadoes
under peculiar moonlight.

That I deserve to feel the whole sky.
That I deserve to feel beyond.

I moved to this city to find myself
in every possible direction.
And I found myself,
I found myself
lying comfortably in the heart of darkness,
between thighs of strangers, in the eyes of
bystanders.
It's surreal—
how my eyes can feel too now!

Shared Spaces and Colliding Worlds

Your right hand looks like the tail of a raccoon, striped in razor cuts and cigarette butts. We also share a room with spiders wearing revenged eyes, while red ants climb on our skin as if they have eyes on us, too. The sound of metal speeding with a late-night subway echoes, reminding us of the front seat passenger called a miserable ghost.

Two planets crash within me when I ask my spirit, "where do you like to live the most" We have lived in a chamber where love spewed like a poisonous air, suffocating us. A room with no mirrors; everyone's eyes would follow us as if we were the most wanted killer.

We also share a cabin with some ravenous shadows, and cats have their eyes on us, too. Our friends have always been an orange-red bulb, and stacks of frozen fans staring at our insides from a broken roof.

Can you hear the sound of train wheels drumming, like the way fragmented stories were screaming at us in our old apartment? Two planets collide into shards of a glass floating in the air, scratching our wounds. I lose my spirit in this infinite doom.

I ask her, "where do you like to live the most?" Under the sky in a bed made of earth, with snails and caterpillars as neighbors? Or under the deep sea where there are no open bruises to allow any entrance for light? No corner for a teensy thought to mold. No space for memories to fold.

I ask you, "where do you like to live the most?"

Mamta

Drifting in the Unknown

A stillness falls upon my distorted face
as my eyes stand static like a mirror,
reflecting the gaze of an unknown world.
My mind wanders in the darkness,
behind cracked, fabricated walls.

Letters disappear.
Thoughts fear losing themselves
in the void forever.
The ticking of every clock stops
as the charcoal sky hits the bottom rock.
A bridge in a faraway town collapse.
Houses sink in the river of agony.
The mountaintop breaks into a million pieces
like hearts.
I find myself standing
under the shade of a million broken stars.
Every.
Corner.
Scarred.

What is this hunger for human bodies,
the touch of animal furs,
and the whisper of a cat's purrs?
It's pouring outside.

Garbage Girl

It's called Rain.
Rain is an illusion.

We are so distant from
the living and breathing these days.
Every apartment has a storage
full of scissors and sleeping pills,
and deranged hills of overwhelming emotions.
Every apartment
has a storage full of imaginary traumas,
new-born dreams,
and extinguished screams.
The light of grief is so powerful to me.
It's blinding
most of the days.

I crawl farther away into the abyss
that lays on top of my chest.
It's called Rain.
Rain is an illusion.
Life is just a delusion.
I surrender
to the art of drifting
into the unknown.

Mamta

AFTER THE ILLUMINATION

"I don't want to know any-thing but this
perpetual wailing, this clatter in the night,
this delay, this infamy, this pursuit,
this inexistence."

– Alejandra Pizarnik
(Translated by Forrest Gander and Patricio Ferrari)

Garbage Girl

DATE: 17/11/2021

Empty streets lead to an empty house, to an empty bedroom, to an empty soul.

Cheers!

'Tis the season of emptiness.

Mamta

Loud Silences

I want to unthink
some flaming memories,
hurting my eyes.

Someone hold my body,
it's falling under deep trenches.
Every particle of my skin floats in the air,
my heart drips on the dusty wooden chair.

I haven't swept my hair in two weeks
from my bedroom floor.
My Ma will kill me if I don't pick up
the pieces of me by midnight.

It's past midnight,
past a million lights,
my hair multiples,
my cries, too.

I am definitely travelling
to an island of the 'sin of my being'.

I want to unfurl
the deceased petals
hurting my mental health.

Noises – an abrupt stop to noises!

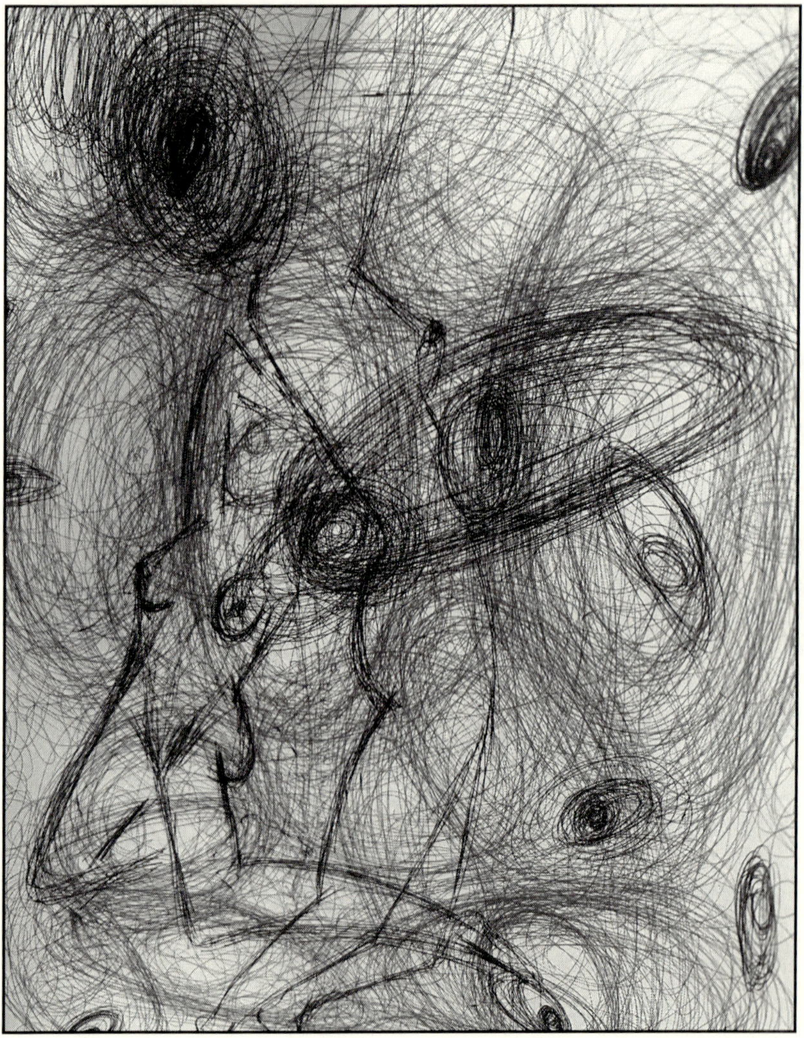

Mamta

Patches

Silently,

This patch of a cloud
Separates like my thighs inside
An abandoned sea beneath
A sea monster

                                      holding me
           greeting me

Like I have never been held   enough
Never been loved   enough
To reach Uranus

They look at me like   I   am   a darted hole
In the middle of a heart

Like I am   a cracked stone
A broken   bone

An overload carriage to this mental world
I would have departed long before   evolution

I still remember I have carved stories
With my   bones   and   blood
And no one cares

No one   cares
About the   battlefield
Heavy emotions circling

I want to find a perfect   hat

Amidst a circus of a   dull life
I sit on a wooden   chair

Garbage Girl

To follow my fantasy   can't wait
To be annihilated by my   abnormality

My   insanity

I   kill   myself   every   single   day

I don't know what it's going to feel like when   I touch
The surface of the sea after   ripping

The sky open I feel   closer
To myself

I want to feel   crunched

In my own body and   squeeze
myself to the heavens

I want to   stretch   my tentacles

And kiss my spine as if I am   a magician

As if   I am   magic

As if I   exist
                                        EXISTED

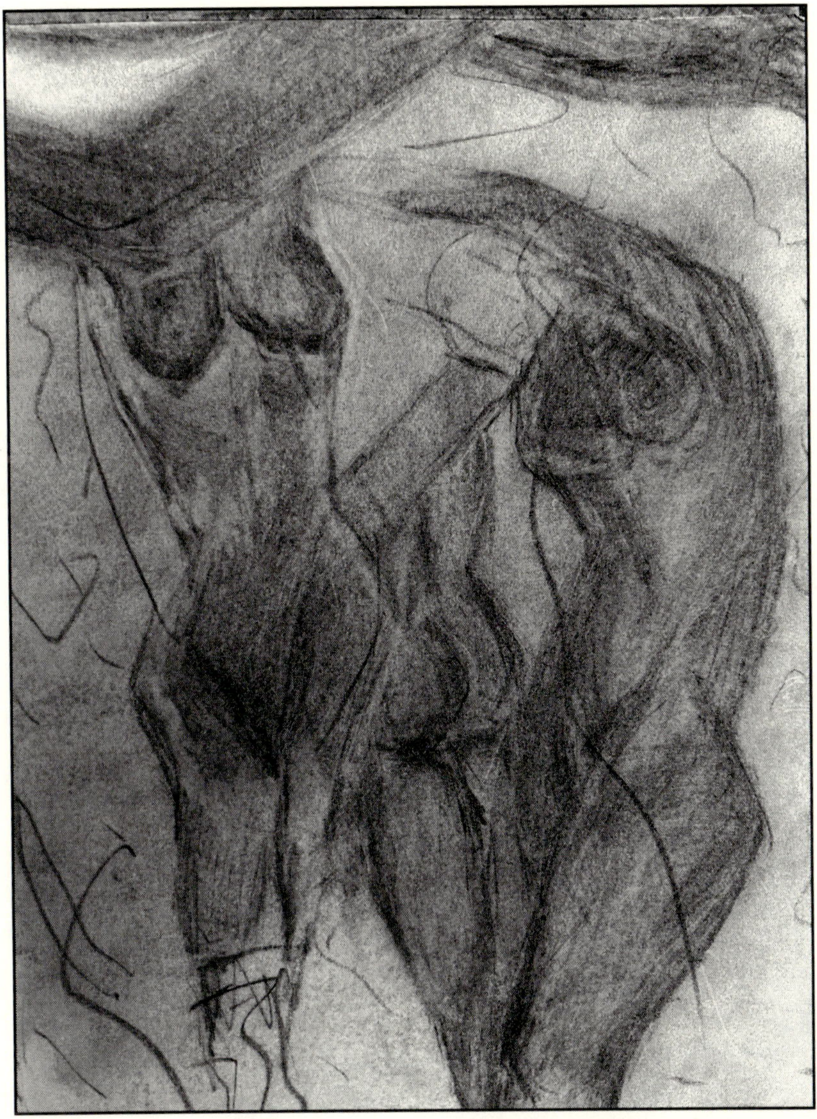

Late October Welcomes the Void:

It's a pungent morning, I think. Grey washed clouds
in late October welcomes the void.
I love sleeping more than living.

All night, I shall listen to the bowels of gloom.
All night, I shall listen to the moans of a heartbroken moon.
Is it the night you love in me?
I become night in the daytime for you.

Vancouver is sad today. It's meant for those in love
who embrace the playfulness of a bitter winter.
The bone marrow of my backyard tree is an illusion
of my memories.

I have died more than I have lived.
I am the cursed winter; people look at me
like I wound them.

I am not a doctor that can heal anyone. I am
a novice creator. I do not want to pain you.
I want to make you feel infinitude.

Mamta

This year's fall is like the fall of empires.
Human hearts are crushed by raging ants.
We are weaving the thread of our disheveled lives.
My body tangles easily these days.
—Just water and dry bones since last May.

What is this? These spiteful words
sprinkled on your mouth like a frightful small-town bird?
Like the only thing we hate in this world is—
this world.

It's a cheerless morning, I think. A long season
to linger in darkness. The walls are inaudible,
like the stillness of the graveyard after midnight
A forbidden flight takes off
as I greet you after the dead of night.

Good morning, love!

Justice for Jared

Walking past thousands of plants in the city,
Waiting for you to lead them home,
Call them pretty and maybe introduce them
To different seasons.

Walking back home on a winter night,
Your mind wanders about drifting lights,
Followed by a mysterious owl
That doesn't need reasons to be awake
During moonlight.

There are snowflakes
On top of the BC lakes.
Your arms feel heartbreaks
In these chilly aches of long winters.

Maybe you could adopt one of the plants
And name them after a dead Jared,
With banners spread throughout the town,
You'll have reasons like me
To come home to someone with a guarantee.

Maybe you could share your horrible day
With the ghost of dead Jared,
Hiding on your window in your dingy,
Gray-blue bedroom.

The feeling of hope is overwhelming.
Just like Jared,
We're all swelling, dwelling in our grief.

Yes, we're all dead, living in disbelief.

Mamta

Looking for You

Metals are braided
into the shape of an unworn necklace.
The shadow of a streetlamp
blooms like a serpentine maze.
Exaggerated hats;
the past is hiding
behind dark sunglasses.

I look for you
amidst the boundless silhouette.
I look for you
amidst the boundless silhouette.
I find you

In the bottom of my coffee mug,
in the shape of half-circled soil.
Muddy paws are climbing
heavy mountains in turmoil,
Carrying the chandelier
of forgiveness –
I am a mess.

I look for you
amidst the boundless silhouette.
I look for you
amidst the boundless silhouette.
I find you.

Garbage Girl

DATE: 04/12/2021

Today,
      I touched the bottom surface within me.

      I saw a giant creature living in a cage
            made of reality. I saw the creature grieving
            over an old graffiti made of constraints
            and imperfections.

      I saw it aching to fly,
            waiting to break free from this tangled
            tree of life, and maybe just maybe,
            build a home in this formidable,
            endless sky.

Mamta

Goodbye Boyfriend

And what do you think about the exploding sun?
I shoved you away last week under the wet soil in a forest,
with memories of your plastic gun from your childhood, Hun.
Why do I have to shelter every broken branch and broken chair
in this neighborhood? All day, I walk with my swollen feet,
and my swollen mind wanders in multiple confined corners.

We wake up to a purpose of building our vessels
and we wait for sin to succumb to us, just to mess us up.
You loved me like a winemaker loves his favorite wine.
But it never stops. Breathing feels like an inhumane crime.

We are all creatures of curiosity, just like cats in the city.
We are all curious to know the secrets of the jungle.
We are all curious to know the scandals of the underwater ocean.
We are all curious to tangle the untangle webs of multiple species.

I swallow my curiosity of flying with monsters
in the vacuum at 3am.
I used to be a night owl; these days,
I don't know what form I should take.
Most days, I want to be a slug in a secret garden.

You, you wanted freedom from the abuse of nature,
so I dragged your body to a secret location
after I murdered you with your plastic gun
from your childhood, Hun.

You smiled at my misery—
I am smiling at your freedom.

Separation in Space

the sun has stained plants
on the back of your right shoulder

your new ink burns tears
under the pearl of your eyes

trout lake has spilled blood
at your new home
on the other side

winds have rolled yellow
on your mountainous ego and pride.

you're here, I'm there
Alas, those were the nights
when we died a million lives

Mamta

Wintering in Vancouver

Bears an unsatisfied appetite
Of burning your tongue
From a rotten coffee,
And the barrenness of
A long evening
Hugs the resident,
Like maggots snuggle
My forlorn grandma's skin
On her graveyard.

I never saw her face one last time
Before she raced her way out
Of this planet. I find myself
Amidst a flavorless crowd
Of a strange species. I think
About an old best friend who isn't
Tight like a rope anymore,
An old lover who isn't
A pretty vermillion ring anymore.

Those painted smiles
Never ended miles,
Streetlamp hisses
Fairy light kisses,
Hearts sinking,
Thoughts burning my skin,
Emotions melting below my chin.

Garbage Girl

Broken bones clattering,
City windows chattering
To an evil darkness.
My newly invested fleece
With the tag of murder fails
To keep my dermis warm,
Only reminding me of
The torture,

& blood,
& bloodline,
& broken spine,
& defeated rhyme
& forgotten mind,
& suffering
& suffering

& suffer…ing.

Mamta

When the Body Splinters into an Interstellar

An extra-terrestrial woman swims in her own filthy,
unlit body. She plunges so hard, her intestines shatter

into a million stellar shards. She finds herself trapped, swinging.

Could someone please explain her how the world is stinging?
Out in the woods, she lies bare on the wet mud,

piercing her tentacles, feeling aches as if earthquakes are

arriving in an old-fashioned fashion.
Her moans sound like the whistles of

another lost planet in a different dimension.

Only shy cats with enchanting eyes can see her insides
shine like magma. She inches closer to the beginning

of suffering. Her flesh melts after winter. She's dying right now,
eternally this time, as her body splinters into an interstellar.

After the Illumination

"Illumination" is the word that came to my mind while lighting a patchouli incense so that I can become transcendental tonight. Every time I listen to an instrumental violin moving like desires in silence, I think about an in-depth longing she carries in her voice. I hear the shrieks of dead people dancing at twilight. As I try to sew my journey for this night, I see rose petals painting the sky, and pale clouds slowly reuniting to enjoy the Festival of Lights.

> My favorite rose petal killed herself to create art with
> a mesmerizing gunshot.

An afternoon ray curls my body like I am a lost princess craving for some warmth. I cannot move an inch today. I read about the tragedies of the birth of mankind and was immersed in the waves of Rimbaud's poetry. A lone rose petal lies on top my favorite poet's grave, as if in a concealed prayer. I promised myself that I will touch my feet to the bottom of the earth's top layer. But my feet refuse to move an inch. They stay paralytic in bed like a dead petal, an unwanted pebble. I stay waiting for some illumination.

> It's finally lit— every corner is warmer for a minute.

DATE: 25/11/2021

Flowers are blooming out of my mouth—
  I'm trying to understand the science behind this mint "madness".
  I am parched today; it's been raining a lot every day.

into the deep

again and again
I ask how deep the grief—
rotten tangerine

I am exhausted
Papa, please take me in—
bones growing deeper

again and again
I ask how hollow sorrow—
deepening apricot

all my tears are dry
on upcoming sorrows and deaths—
the deepest nightmare

again and again
the waning crescent moon shares
a void so deep

all my screams deeper—
eyes, bones, blood are now aching
ribs are now breaking

again and again
I ask how deep new wound—
darkening oranges

where do I go now?
this old house is deepening
broken wings fluttering

Mamta

In Time,

I follow my father's kind heart
after my ribs have parted inch by inch,
my soul has departed to this new world where
my body hides under the corner of my bed, as if
my body feels nauseated from breathing toxic air, as if
my body feels suffocated for running away from my father's
cozy lair.

In time,

I follow my mother's loveable eyes
after my arms have broken into pieces,
my nose bleeds *drip, drip, drip* on a wooden crib,
forgotten long creases of my dusty skin,
my name withers away,
my soul jitters on a rusty ashtray,
my heart crunches my foreign lies
as I stay hidden in the corner
of my mother's eyes.

FUNERAL SEASON

*"I am nobody; I have nothing to do with explosions.
I have given my name and my day-clothes up to the nurses
And my history to the anaesthetist and my body to surgeons".*

- Tulip by Sylvia Plath

Mamta

The Light of Grief

> If only grief finds a corner to rest and be honest,
> And accept its flaw, live fully, feel holy —
> There would be nothing in this world
> As beautiful as experiencing grief
> In its entirety.

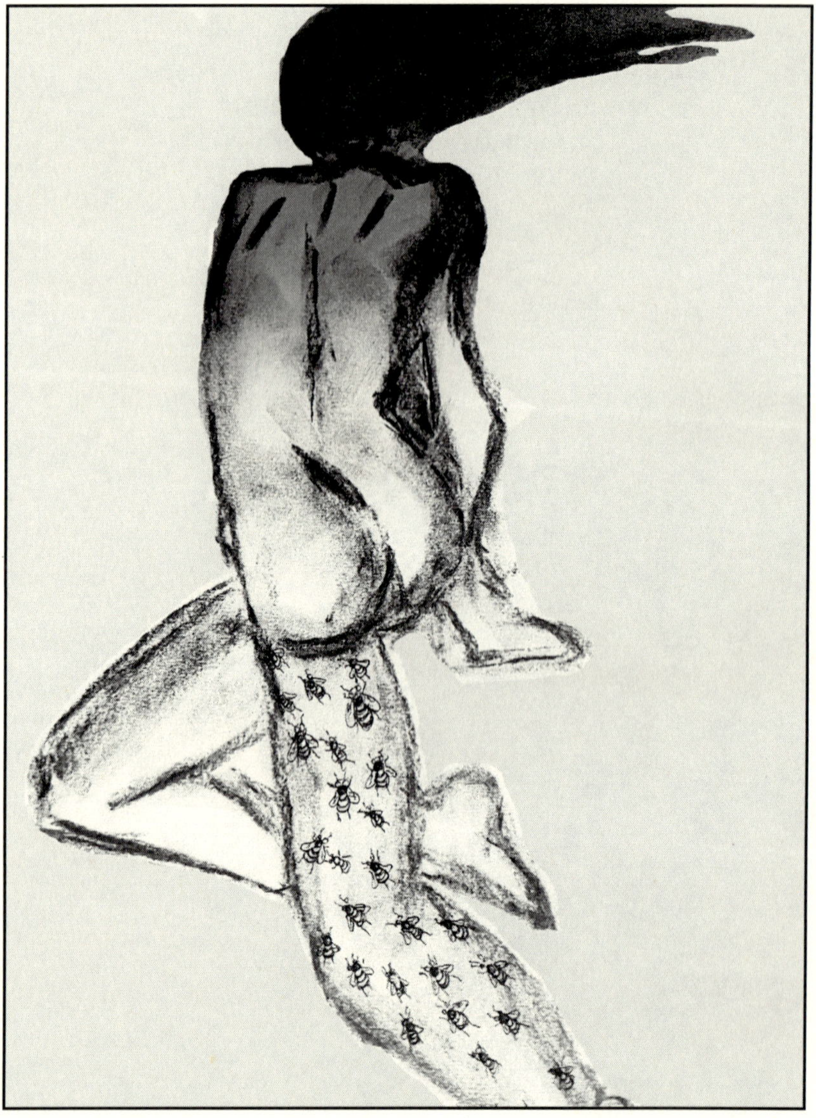

Mamta

Forgotten Days

What day is it today? I think it's Monday, but I don't know if it's really Monday today. I forget about days as easily as ruptured eyes forget about my unstructured face. It's as if my cat forgets to turn off the flush in the toilet. And my doormat forgets about reality, while all we perceive is a gray abstract monster swaying to the rhythms of The Cranberries in an old coffee shop.

My day stretches like two men staring at the sun-kissed ground, and their glowing printed shirts takes round on Commercial Drive. I also think about the textured sweat of the blue brick building opposite to JJ Bean, sitting on my chest for days now. I smell like an overgrown potato, with roots sprouting out of my body. It reminds me of my medieval layers concealing my modern skin, as if it wants to hide me from playing flute on the street. Like that woman with rectangular glasses making sweet sounds with the air for a spare change outside JJ Bean on a sunny day. And my day screams at me, as if I am ashamed to remember my Ma's faded dreams that also screams in extreme agony of being born in a womb. I forget about the eternal gloom of existence, of breathing this toxic, toxic air that also disappears under a middle-aged man's hair, crossing the same street and walking farther away from my eyes.

No one cares if I walk out of a group conversation. I bought a citrine ring yesterday. Or was it on Wednesday, maybe? I thought it would blend with my long antler-like fingers for Friday night. I ran away on my imaginary boat and climbed as far as I could today. My body has limitations. We passed out for twelve hours under this earth, beside snails, blanketed in dirt. There should be a purpose to waking up. I feel purposeless like a tangerine dress going for a walk on a tangerine day. It doesn't make any sense to stay where we are not needed. I had to run away with myself to save myself from myself, a part that is not a real part of myself, and it's making me hate myself to say this, but I want to enjoy the art of being myself today.

And then I wither away in the middle of a conversation about Chlamydia, with my three friends, over a few Coronas, and suffer alone on the top berth of an illusory train, hiding my brain like a clone. Of course, I have had UTI; I can't purr all the time because I don't feel love anymore.

"Sunday evenings can get busy," says a cute barista. I stay with solitude splashed in my favorite cup of coffee, and her smile echoes in the corner of an old coffee shop. I am not alone any more like a forgotten day, perhaps a Monday, perhaps a doomsday.

Mamta

Unearthing in Alleyways

Orange stripes in Vancouver led me to a boulevard that belongs to a dead artist. I swallowed my soul for breakfast. I wandered in an alley for a while, searching for a comfortable corner beside the coffin of a dead poet with a faded smile. Just so you know, it's all about my demented mind.

Yellow flowers, a yellow taste circling on my tongue, a yellow day; sad, sad humans astray. Ions and ions of agony lurking beneath a little girl's eyes. A yellow cab just surrendered, while innocent mice met their demise. I see mountains in the distance, wearing hats to hide their face. Everyone wants to hide their cat's face today. I have been hiding mine my entire life. I hide my yellow-shaped breasts behind my 8-year-old body. I hide the right one, for she is the most vulnerable. I wish I were as strong as the left one. I wish I desired her curiosity to battle. She loves the most, I believe. I hide my purple thighs, my charcoal black eyes, my circular disguise.

I follow people wearing black jackets, black socks, black comets, black vomit. Trees are ready to attend the most-awaited wedding of this spring. I, on the other hand, yearn to depart on the back of a departing wind. Another stranger with a distorted vision asks for my name. I forget my name. Humans ask me my name as if I'm part of an unwanted game. The heart behind my right breast roars. What is my name? What is the name of my game? What is the name of this city where my ghost meanders? The stranger's yellow eyes remind me of the terrors of being born as a girl. I am no longer scared of the hailstorm. What is the name of my name, my name is…

Garbage Girl

Painted hair is mesmerizing. I find my corneas stuck on an unborn flare in the alleyway. I loathe the wailing of a baby; it makes me want to rip off my ears. My kidney begs me to be hauled; I get a spine curvature disorder. My nose pours crimson rain. Sometimes, green vomit cascades from my mouth as my bone spikes out of my knee to protect me. My existence unfurls a crimson shame.

My name is litter.

My name is thunder.

My name is...my name is...

An illicit train.

My name is debris.

A perennial stain.

My name is, my name is my name is...

What is my name?

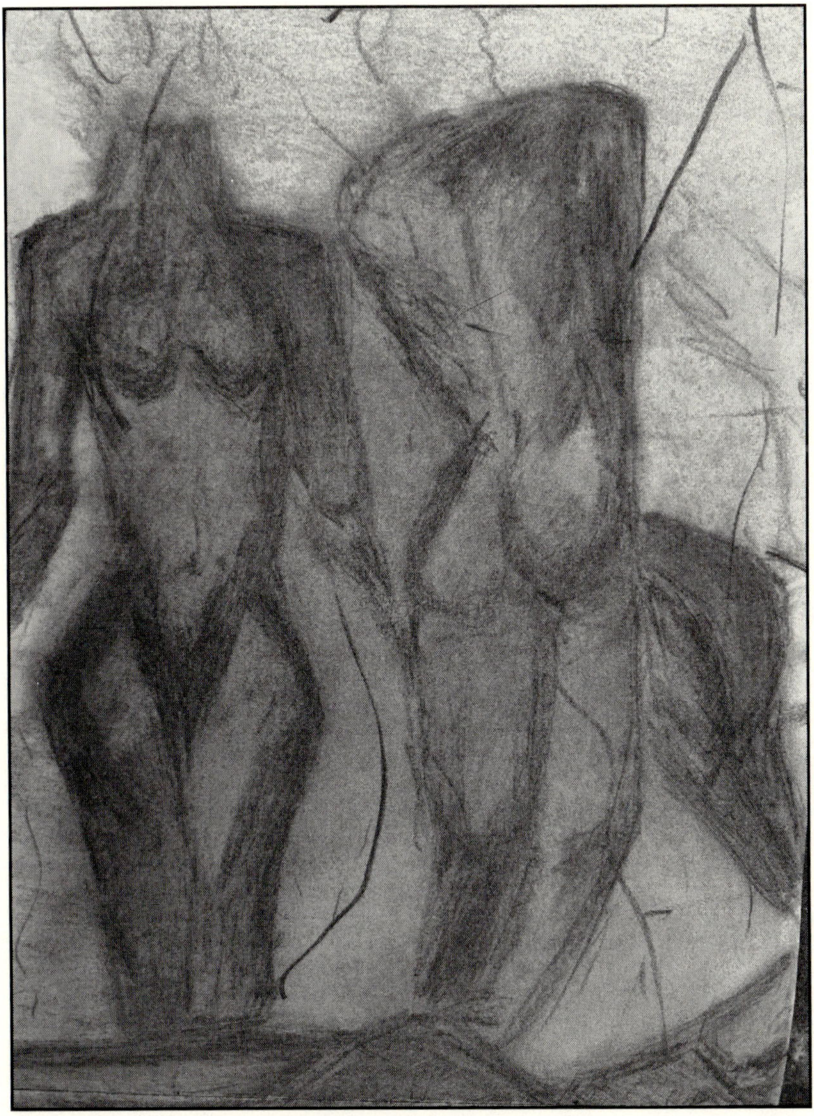

Laughter Season

> Why can't I laugh
>
> The way fireflies laugh at midnight,
>
> Showing off sparkles stuck between their teeth,
>
> And shadows laugh inside hanging mirrors that breathe,
>
> Spiders laugh, sprinting on miserable bodies,
>
> And dead plants laugh at fractured ones
>
> Who can't pick up their dust, and exotic creatures
>
> Living in the garbage bin laugh, munching on the vomit
>
> That I gifted while exhibiting my guilt that also laugh
>
> When I am glued to my linens, smelling like gutter
>
> Molded in another rotten memory that
>
> Also laugh at me for not laughing
>
> the way I am supposed to.
>
> Why can't I just laugh?

Mamta

Where Do the Most Painful Cries Reside?

Piercing through the valley of desires,
Slicing some old wounds,
Meandering alone in this cool night,
Are you even afraid of this blinding light?

We shed our skin,
For the love of torturous sleep,
I know I am that woman,
I should be saving myself from
Sinking in the deepest deep.

Our sweat smells like ice,
With the snowstorm melting in our bones,
And spines.

Between our thighs,
Is where the most painful cries reside.

Garbage Girl

Scars of Two Cities

She devours me, beneath me. Howling screams echo under the first light of another day.

Trees in Vancouver are clothed again. I sit undressed in the middle of an abandoned street, swallowing my green vomit as rain cascades on top of my black hair, which I packed as a souvenir from Bombay in a spare bag. Bombay doesn't talk to me anymore. She has many travelers now. Bombay can't breathe now.

I have walked on my knees to get rid of her solid clutch. I broke my pigtail attempting to squeeze my head to forget and forget. I try to forget the screams of street vendors strolling in my childhood lane. I try to forget the little girl with a red face, wearing red pyjamas, crying red rivers, hiding her deep red quivers. I try to forget the green religious temples shutting ears to free prayers. I broke my volume attempting to squeeze my ears to forget and forget. Bombay is hiding her scars behind her thick, brown brows. Bombay is suffocating now.

      I also try to forget the orange society
    and their orange, ugly frog faces from the past
      which I packed as a souvenir for Vancouver.
        I try to forget the navy holocaust
    that disfigured the little girl's body and soul.

        Screams are different in Vancouver.
     Most days, she moans like a searing rain
        canoodling with historical pain.

          Some days, she sounds
        like the deadliest silence
      suppressed under the corners of
      an ancient sea like a foreigner.

    Vancouver is hiding her new scars
      behind her thick, black brows.
    Vancouver can't stop crying now.

Existential Crisis

I exist

    Like nitrogen in the air,
    My color is translucent.
    I come from an unexplored side of the universe
    Beyond the Milky way,
    Beyond dark matter.

        I lay in the bed of a floating ballroom,
        A floating doe walking around the river,
        A floating baby elephant splashing in the ocean,
        A floating heart of my old self plunging in an old well.

            I lay for fourteen hours,
            For fourteen years,
            Fourteen pieces of my heart
            Are now a part of the constellation.

                Who am I?

Poisoned Rats

Looking
For my sad, notorious child,
A piece of mine, lost and exiled,
Hiding under the knots of my curly hair.

I wasn't aware of what she needs,
I wasn't aware of how she breathes.

I will rip open the sky.
Don't cry, baby girl.

I am learning the maps of this new city.
We are scared,
We are fractured—
An unfortunate lump of this universe.
We are scattered
Like poisoned rats
Looking for a home.

But thankfully, our refuge is interlaced
In the knots of my curly hair.
We are both safely tangled
In this immortal despair.

Mamta

I Can't Pick Myself Up

I trudge through shallow waters, burdened
by my nightmare of surviving another hour.
I open my arms and wait for the mystics
to sprinkle electrical power on my weakened paws.
I haven't lost my body yet; I try to forgive myself
for torturing my fingers again and again.
Only because I offer love sometimes.
Most of the time, I offer stings as my ghost sings
about the sins of my being.
I am only trying to understand the dirt of living life,
but all I have been offered is a sharp knife
to dig comfort in an abstract void.

I can't pick myself up.

I dissolve into thin air.
I know I am not a necromancer.
I am a broken-winged bird,
seeking illicit answers.
I dissolve into thin despair.

I know how it all started,
how the earth was formed,
how plants were born,
how we die,
how we heal,
die,
heal,
dying,
healing.

I can't pick myself up.

Hunger Games

Do I know what it feels like to be free?
All my life, I have been imprisoned beneath
A concrete asylum with some mad species.
I learned madness on my own,
Crawling every night hunting alone.
But never found flesh that tastes like a Mammoth,
But never found flesh of sunbeams and black hole.

I have been hungry for years now,
Fading away like charred coal.
My obsession of sharpening my teeth
To pass these hours of my life takes a bite
Of anything citrine.
I don't know any other way,
Just like I don't know how it feels
To be free-spirited and free my spirit
Once and for all
From life's struggle,
From eating hearts in trouble.

Hunger.
Emptiness.
I die of starvation every day.

Mamta

Eternal Decay

Since when did brushing my teeth
feel like a monotonous job that I hate?
I am tired of cleaning my grim memories
again and again and again,

and it doesn't excite me anymore
to smell fresh like mint.
Maybe I am meant to be tinted.

I am meant to decay.

I am meant to be cemetery.

Nausea

I want to vomit me out
Every bit of
Existence breathing.

Inside me, I am hatching
Like ants crawling
Out of my mouth.
How much loving?

This home is not mine.

Mountains mutter at night.
If only I weren't so afraid,
If only there was a home,

I would be happy, all alone.

Mamta

Numbing

I see a seashore melting beneath my bones,
Behind the doors, my gut shivers like cold stones.

How can I find depth in this summer?
I wish the cold weather would stay longer
To repair my bruises like an uncalled plumber.

I wait for summer every year,
But today, I am happy that it's chilly here.
My heart is freezing, and I feel the skin of
An arctic flourishing like a lily,
That my father never prayed for.

I feel what a fully shaved polar bear must be feeling.
I feel what a distant whale must be feeling.
I feel what an infant penguin must be feeling.

It's a good feeling, trust me,
When you open your arms and let the frosty air
Numb your heart,
Your misery,
You.

Burial Process

I buried my bones last night
after shedding my skin on a turf,
begging for a mysterious tiger
to windsurf with me on the shore.

Tigers hid all night. I encountered
blue smoke and a mule deer
curiously waiting for my existence
to clear away.

I cried for someone to eat
my remaining parts. I cried for spirits
to feast on my leftover heart.
I cried for forgiveness.

There was a power cut in my old city.
I slowly picked up the broken stone
and hid away from this gritty life.
I cried inside my barren womb —
it poured like a mourning tomb.

Mamta

Grandma's Final Prime

When does it end?
She asks before her midnight amends,
lying on the same rectangular bed each day,
obeying her final dreams and nightmares,
slowly fading into a million flares.
Following the darkness, she counts her time.

Tik Tok, Tik Tok. How does it end?

She questions her universe while ascending
into tales of war heroes and blending her body
in holy books. Gazing at twilight colors one last time,
skies and human faces blur, transferring
into the last minute that just passed. She inquires about the time.

Tik Tok, Tik Tok, Tik Tok. Where does it end?

Amidst the war
between living and the monster called death,
awaiting at her door, she lies snug under her blanket,
sniffing dust and wind that might not exist in the ditch,
begging to unstitch her soul, to be born anew.

She no longer wishes to mourn about cancer's grip,
chewing her time with open eyes, relishing her final prime,
singing like a nightingale one last time.

Tik Tok, Tik Tok, Tik. When does it end?

Garbage Girl

I Smell Like the Whiff of a Hospital Bathroom, Covered in the Vomit of a Cancer Patient

An unbearable breeze carried news
of a freshly built grave, and the owner,
whom I happened to know once,
has decided to surrender themselves
as an ordinary slave.

A sandalwood incense lay dead
on my bedside table.
Cinders were strewn.
My body is feeling parched
in the middle of a salty dune.

Each time, I take a whiff outside my blanket,
the list of dead people climbs the loudest cliff.
As if death is a heartless bitch.

I caress my bandages,
I smell like medicines,
and sleeping pills.

My Ma and Pa are aging.
My heart is raging today.
As I sniff my armpits,
they smell like blood squeezed
from plastic syringes.
And fresh marks of brutality
on my skin now stings.

I smell like warm urine
on freshly laundered linen.
I smell like a public hospital.

Mamta

Little by little,
death acts like a ruthless bitch.
When I am the one ready to surrender,
there's always a glitch.

That bitch!
That bitch!

Monstrous Urge

And the monster in me expands
through the door of my spine,
quivers.

I broke my left hand's wrist,
my veins reminded me of
the blood loss during the incision
performed by a little girl
wearing my body.

I slap my face so tight,
it looks like a raging moon tonight.
My failed attempt to possess
this whole body
burns too.

No need to survive,
clawed marks of insecurity
on my neck now shines.
I broke my knees to kneel
in front of the divine.

Nothing, nothing can replace
the sensation of a knife
piercing my body
like a distant lover
piercing my soul —
pleasant and barbaric.

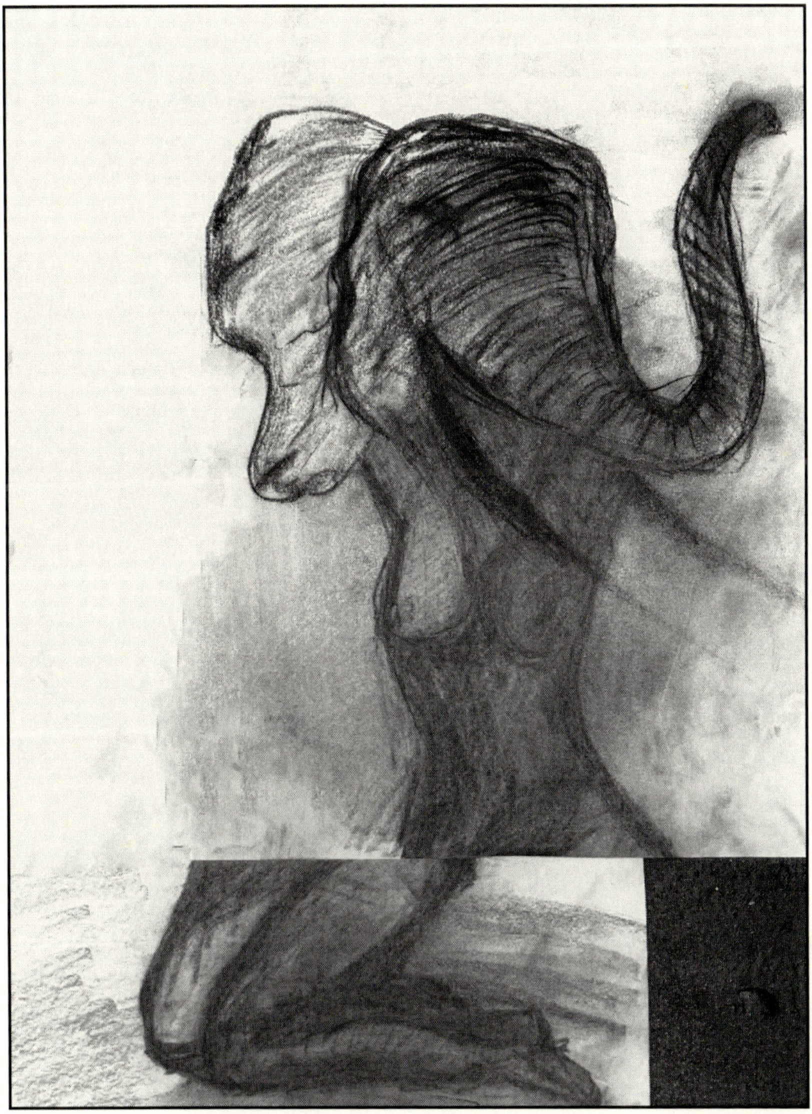

Funeral Season

Tornadoes sang transcendental songs at dawn.
Ashes lie strewn on the skin of a faraway ocean,
Prayers untold, wishes unfold,
Unexplored mind wandered; nightmares also roared.

My bottom lip is thicker like the fog tonight.
How does it matter if lips smile?
Or quiver in fear? I drown in the gutter beside
a dead deer; dreams also roared.

Funerals are not meant to be happy.
They're sad. So sad. Sadder than
the survival of the planet Earth.
Sadder than any ordinary human birth.
Sadder than just a blistered knee.
Broken me feels so, so, sad.

I wake up grieving the loss of
my body to ugly nights. I smell like
a burnt incense, a burnt toast
perfectly done, and even ghosts
wait to gnaw on me in their graveyard.

But I don't want to be a feast anymore.
I want to smell like a woman who bathes in
lavender. I want to taste like citrus.
I want to feel
like an ice-cream, maybe a potato,
blueberries too.

But today, I smell like a funeral,
I taste like a funeral,
I feel like a funeral.

Two

The winds of Bombay traveled with me two years ago. The skies opened their arms for me two weeks ago. My body started to crack like an old clothing rack two days ago. My eyes are wide close, my lips are bound like a forbidden blue rose, my ears are wide open.

I think about the rancid smell of local trains in Bombay, I reminisce about the sweet, earthy scent of monsoon rains from my childhood. As I cloak myself in never-ending summers, I don't know how it feels like. Is it time to fly again? Our bodies have started to cry, again. Should we break the relationships that we know? It's time to row the boat, don't start slow. We've got to work for our first biggest show. We should erase the map; we should stay away from the trap of searching for home.

Killing souls and picking up the ashes together —
I swirl with Bombay rain to break the chain of captivity.
After all, Bombay is a garbage girl.

A red velvet lamp stands like a vintage hat behind a stranger's head. I think about the lonely bed that I left unmade. I let myself sink in a valley of guilt. Can someone unbraid my hair? I reminisce about the crows in Vancouver disappearing like silvery smoke. As I cloak myself in never-ending winters, I don't know how it feels like.

Is it time to move again? Our hearts have started to ache again. Should we leave the directions that we know? It's time to row the boat, don't start slow. We should erase the map; we should stay away from the trap of searching for home. Killing and picking up the ashes together. I swirl with Vancouver rain to break the chain of captivity.

After all, Vancouver is a garbage girl.

Garbage Girl

Cold has found its direction to my heart. Haven't we glued our broken fingers a million times already? As I cloak myself in never-ending seasons, I don't know how it feels like. This feeling, when the abandoned asteroids battle and rattle beneath my belly. This feeling, when my knees are paralyzed after I catch the breath of hidden mountains staring at me like an uninvited death. I wonder if they are having a conversation about me.

I wonder if they think I am a fool, and a fool, and an extremely foolish woman to run away. I wonder if they snicker at me and think I am a lost debris.

Do they think,

I am a foul litter, an unwanted grey glitter.
I am a bitter soap, an intertwined rope.
Swirling with an unstoppable rain, I break the chain of
captivity.
After all, I am a garbage girl.
After all, we are garbage girls.

Pat on Your Back

Why do you dwell in darkness?
    When light simmers within you,
        It splatters in a million little hues.

        What is this unspeakable desire?
            That lives in the rims of your house,
                Camouflaged in the moods of nature.

            Red roses are dying.
                Are you even living enough?
                    Climbing is tough, how do you
                    do it?

incomplete circles

it feels pointless some days waiting
                the sun to paint red on your lips quivering

it feels poisonous some hours lying
                the roof on top of your eyes hanging

it feels satisfying some nights defeating
                a stranger's compliment circling

it feels depressing some seconds losing
                an old self on your new skin melting

it feels soothing some hours drowning
                your newest heart burning

it feels tranquilizing some years knowing
                your classical fantasies flourishing

it feels fascinating some time learning
                your every muscle dancing

it feels illuminating some lives craving
                your every particle of love lamenting

it feels useless some days waiting
                the moon to glow within you self-isolating

it feels cheating some ions dreaming
                incomplete circles of life looming

Still Alive

Do you like to caress splinters on my body
After midnight? I sleep like the night sky
With my injured skin resting on your pillow.
I don't want a lover's kiss to wake up,
I don't believe any king or queen can heal me.
Battle of waves, listen to my prayers,
The only thing that can save me from myself is
The zesty taste of lemonade traveling down my raspy throat,
Comforting me like I deserve to be comforted.

Do you see the night in me
Layered in a withered moon?
I sleep like a nightmare
On days when there is no escape,
I drench my body three times
In the pool where the last sunset crimes,
I exhibit my bruises to the Holy chimes.

Here goes the truck full of sadness,
Brimming with rejected raindrops.
Expired leaves in my backyard are weeping,
I also hear the mourning of an apple tree dancing
With an overzealous wind calling my name.
I can't be free anymore.

I scream,
I am alive,
Just like aching flames,
I am alive,
Just like deceased remains,
I am alive,
Just like abandoned spaces,

Garbage Girl

I am alive,
Like ruptured places,
I am alive,

I am alive.

Mamta

एक दर्द ऐसा भी

"कहो तो थोड़ा वक़्त भेज दूँ, सुना है तुम्हें फुर्सत नहीं मुझसे मिलने की।"

- Gulzar

ऐसा वक्त

१)

एक वक्त ऐसा भी आया की
तुम्हे हर रोज ना देखूँ
कभी सोचा नहीं था।

एक वक्त ऐसा भी आया की
तुम्हे हर रोज ना सुनु
कभी सोचा नहीं था।

एक वक्त ऐसा भी आया की
तुम्हे आखरी बार
शमशान मे मिलूँ
कभी सोचा नहीं था।

२)

एक तूफान ऐसा आया
कि हमारा घर छीन लिया
जिसका कोई गम नहीं।

एक तूफान ऐसा आया
कि हमारी रूह छीन ली
जिसका भी कोई गम नहीं।

पर एक तूफान ऐसा आया
कि तुम्हारी ज़िंदगी छीन ली
और हमें गंदगी समझ कर
इस कचरे जैसे दुनिया में नम छोड़ दिया
गम की परछाई के साथ।

Garbage Girl

ऐसा कैसे हो गया

ऐसा कैसे हो गया
इसका जवाब तो कभी नही मिलेगा
पर अब हो गया
ना तुम आओगे
ना तुम्हे बुला सकती हूँ
बस घर से निकलूँगी तो सिर्फ तुम्हे ढूंढने के लिए।

ना तुम आओगे
ना तुम्हे बुला सकती हूँ
फिर भी घर से निकलूँगी तो सिर्फ तुम्हे ढूंढने के लिए।

छोड़ दी यह पृथ्वी हमने तुम्हारे लिए
अब लेकर चलो उस जहान में
जहा सिर्फ तुम हो
और मैं, पापा।
जिसके बिना तुम्हारी सांसें भी सांस नही लेती थे
और अब वही सांसें रूठी हुई हमसे क्यु, पापा।

Mamta

लेकर चलो उस जहान में
जहा सिर्फ तुम हो
और मैं, पापा।

दम घूट रहा है तुम्हारे बिना
अकेले से भी ज्यादा अकेला महसूस हो रहा है।

ऐसा कैसे हो गया
इसका जवाब तो मैं लेकर ही रहूँगी, पापा।

खोयी खोयी

अब तो खोयी खोयी रहती हूँ
तुम्हें ढूँढ़ती रहती हूँ
पथरों में
आसमान में
दरबार में
पर तुम ना आए इस बार

इसलिए हमने बना दिया
एक घर तुम्हारे कब्र के बाहर।

Mamta

दर्द की बारिश

इस दुनिया में कोई भी चीज हमें दर्द नहीं दे सकती।

अब तो हमे रास्ते पर ला दोगे।
तो भी चिट्टी के काटने जितना दर्द नहीं होगा।

अब तो हमारी रूह भी छीन लोगे
तो भी रेत के फिसलने जितना दर्द नहीं होगा।

अब तो प्रलय भी आ जाए
और पैरों से जमीन भी खिसक जाए
और आकाश भी साथ छोड़ दे
तो भी दिल टूटने का दर्द नहीं होगा।

करके आये गुस्सा उस खुदा को
जिसने ऐसा दर्द की बारिश दी
कि अब दर्द का महाप्रलय भी आ जाए
तो भी दर्द नहीं होगा।

नाराजगी

१)

ऐसा महसूस हो रहा है कि
आत्मा शरीर से नाराज है
शरीर सांसों से नाराज है
साँसें आँसुओं से नाराज है
आंसू रब से नाराज है
रब जिंदगी से नाराज है
जिंदगी कायनात से नाराज है
कायनात हमारे वजूद से नाराज है
और हम
हम सिर्फ तुमसे नाराज हैं।

२)

आजकल डर लगता है
इन सांसों से
जिनको बुलाया नहीं
फिर भी आ जाती है
बिन बुलाए मेहमान की तरह
और परेशान करती है
बिन बुलाए अरमान की तरह।

कहां चले गए तुम
क्यों चले गए तुम
इतना भी क्यों नाराज थे हमसे
कसम से
यह जीवन छोड़कर चले गए तुम।

बस हुआ अब

बस हुआ अब
नहीं जीना अब
नहीं जीना अब
बस हुआ, कब आओगे अब?

लेके चलो अपने साथ
एक बात कहनी थी
लेके चलो उस पार
उस रात जो आखिरी थी हमारे साथ।

बस हुआ अब
नहीं जीना अब
नहीं जीना अब
बस हुआ, कब आओगे अब?

ऐ मन

ऐ मन
तू इतना क्यों नाराज है उस रब से
जिसने तुझे सब से ज्यादा दिया
और जो तुझे सबसे ज्यादा प्यारी थी
वो भी छीन लिया
बस यह कह कर
अब तू अकेले ही मर
अब तू अकेले ही मर।

ऐ मन
तू इतना क्यों नाराज है उस रब से
जिसने तुझे सब से ज्यादा मान दिया
और जो तुझे जान प्यारी थी
वो भी छीन लिया
बस यह कह कर
अब यह हमारी है
अब यह हमारी है।

ऐ मन
तू इतना क्यों नाराज है उस रब से
अब तो उसने तेरी जमीन भी छीन ली
बस यह कह कर
यकीन कर मुझ पर
बस यकीन कर।

Garbage Girl

ऐ मन
तू इतना क्यों नाराज है उस रब से
जिसने तेरी फलक तक छीन लिया

बस तेरे एक झलक का इंतजार है
अब तो कोई डर नहीं
बस मर भी जाए
तो कोई फिक्र नहीं
कोई फिक्र नहीं।

Notes & Acknowledgements

"Garbage Girl" came into being during the two-year span from 2020 to 2022, a time when my Canadian visa restricted me from returning to my hometown of Bombay. The collection predominantly comprises my random thoughts, visuals, memories expressed in the stream of consciousness format, penned before retiring to bed. There was a phase in my life when even stepping outside my bed felt like an arduous task. And that's when the book was born in my personal bedroom and space after 25 years that presented me an opportunity to articulate my emotions without interruption.

The title, "Garbage Girl," originated from an incident during my time as a production assistant for the locations department on a film set. Among my duties was the task of cleaning up rubbish. I vividly recall conducting one final sweep at the end of the day when a colleague asked me to locate the truck while he attempted to move it. Overhearing my supervisor speaking, I misinterpreted his words, thinking he had referred to me as the "garbage girl" due to the trash in my hand. Curiously, I approached him and asked, "Did you call me garbage girl?" He replied with a no, and I chuckled, saying, "I thought I heard that." He responded wryly, "I'm the garbage boy." Since he was literally driving a rubbish truck to dispose of for the set. To which I retorted, "Well, I am a garbage girl. We are all garbage people." That moment struck me, encapsulating the essence of what this book represents.

I would like to express my gratitude to two individuals who are my entire world and who have enabled me to pursue my dreams. My mother, Anita Sunil Nagpal, who devoted her life to taking care of my brother and me since she was 17. She has never ventured outside the city by herself yet trusted me to leave the country independently. Thank you, Ma, for the world you give me each day.

Garbage Girl

I don't even know how to thank my father, Sunil N Nagpal, in person, as he departed from this world a few months ago. If it weren't for his faith and strength in granting freedom to his youngest daughter in this patriarchal world, I wouldn't be where I am today. He treated me no differently than my brother. His belief in me has been a driving force in where I stand today. Thank you, Papa, for being my guarding angel and my guiding light.

I want to express my gratitude to my two best friends. Dainish Agnani, who has consistently provided comfort during my moments of anxiety at the most unexpected hours of the day, and who manages to make me feel at home despite the miles that separate us.

And to Kayla Brix, who has consistently encouraged me to be unapologetically myself, and has been the primary reason I felt comfortable openly discussing my mental health. Thank you both.

Thank you, Jordon Emans, for allowing me to use the title "Wintering in Vancouver" for one of my poems. You've been one of my closest friends since my early days in Vancouver and a significant catalyst for my writing journey.

I am truly thankful for having my brother, Nitin Nagpal, and my sister-in-law, Saachi Nagpal, in my life. Their beautiful gift, Devin Nagpal, continues to bring happiness and new light to my life.

Thank you to the poets for unprecedented inspiration, including Sylvia Plath, Arthur Rimbaud, Aase Berg, and Alejandra Pizarnik. I would also like to thank Maya Angelou for being my poetic inspiration in my early days.

Mamta

Finally, in the wake of my father's passing, grief became a new companion, wrapping itself around my every thought and shadowing my every step. The most painful part is that I couldn't even see his body and his face in person during his funeral, and this regret will stay with me for the rest of my life. It was in this moment of profound loss and vulnerability that a new form of expression found its way to me – Hindi poetry. These Hindi verses intertwined seamlessly with the themes of the original collection, compelling me to include them at the last moment, even after the completion of the collection.

ABOUT THE AUTHOR

Leave me alone.
Don't ask me my name
As if my name is going to heal you,
Conceal your pain.
My words will only serve to remind you
Of your torture and disdain.

I don't belong here,
But I hail from Mumbai,
The city of dreams, as they say.
I've only heard suppressed screams,
Following me to Vancouver,
Where I dwell,
Enveloped in greens—
The city of despair,
Nothing left to repair.
I don't belong here.

I belong to the peculiar sky,
Since poetry found its way
Into my eye a decade ago.
I belong to the unhinged asteroids
That glow during the darkest nights.
I might build a boat and sail
Above the clouds
To find my father on second Earth,
But my birth mother waits for me here,
I live beneath the tragic sea.
I love to disappear.

Mamta

This is me.
Through pages, my soul breathes.
I find my voice amidst the broken wreaths,
Mounted on her naked canvas.
Life feels like a mess.
I find it difficult to express dialogues,
And thus, my escapism lies in
Surrealism, and absenteeism,
Breathing for visual dreams
within the realm of Cinema.
I find solace in flawed creation.
Flawed constellation.
In isolation, I find myself.
I find myself in isolation.

Leave me alone.
Let me linger in the shadows,
In the unknown.

– Mamta Sunil Nagpal

All interior artwork and cover page artwork
in this publication are exclusively created by
Mamta Sunil Nagpal.
Copyright © 2024 Mamta Sunil Nagpal.
All rights reserved.
Unauthorized reproduction or distribution is prohibited.

Manufactured by Amazon.ca
Acheson, AB